Everything Is Changing

Carmel Reilly
Cheryl Orsini

Australia • Brazil • Japan • Korea • Mexico • Singapore • Spain • United Kingdom • United States

Everything Is Changing

Fast Forward

Orange Level 15

Text: Carmel Reilly
Illustrations: Cheryl Orsini
Editor: Kate McGough
Design: Karen Mayo
Series design: James Lowe
Production controller: Emma Hayes
Audio recordings: Juliet Hill, Picture Start
Spoken by: Matthew King and Abbe Holmes

ISBN 978 0 17 012598 7
ISBN 978 0 17 012597 0 (set)

Cengage Learning Australia
Level 7, 80 Dorcas Street
South Melbourne, Victoria Australia 3205
Phone: 1300 790 853

Cengage Learning New Zealand
Unit 4B Rosedale Office Park
331 Rosedale Road, Albany, North Shore NZ 0632
Phone: 0800 449 725

For learning solutions, visit **cengage.com.au**

Printed in Australia by Ligare Pty Ltd
10 11 12 13 14 15 16 19 18 17 16 15

Evaluated in independent research by staff from the Department of Language, Literacy and Arts Education at the University of Melbourne.

Everything Is Changing

Carmel Reilly
Cheryl Orsini

Contents

10th May, 1934

It was my birthday yesterday.
I turned thirteen, and I got three things.

The first was a cake that Mum made.
She had to go next door to use the oven
because we don't have one in our house.
But it turned out all right.
In fact, I think it was the best cake
I've ever had.

10th May, 1934

The second thing I got was
this notebook.
My dad gave it to me.
He said I will need to use it
to keep track of my life now.

I didn't understand what Dad meant
until he told me what the third thing was.

He had found a job for me.

10th May, 1934

Chapter 2

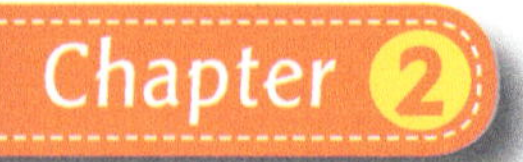

14th May, 1934

Today, I started working for a man who makes houses.
I am really lucky to get a job like this, with such a good boss.

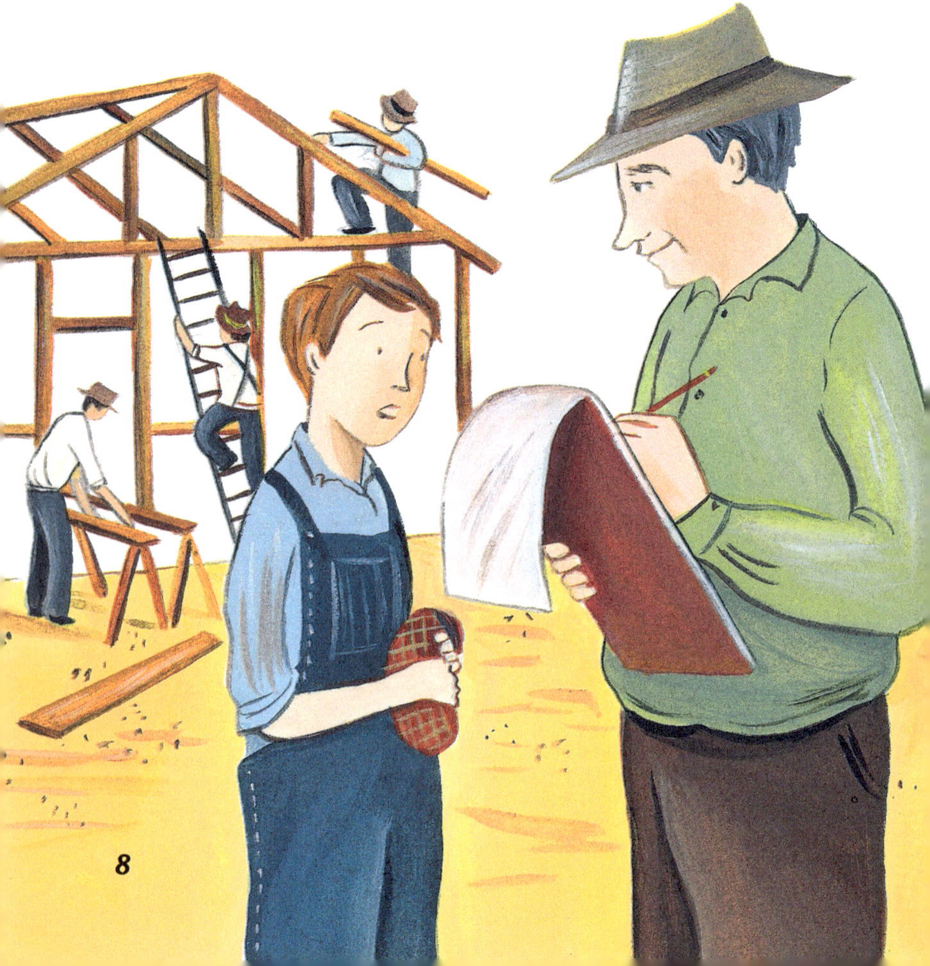

This notebook is for keeping track
of my pay and the hours I work.
But I want to use it to write down
things about my life,
because everything is changing
so fast now.

Chapter 3

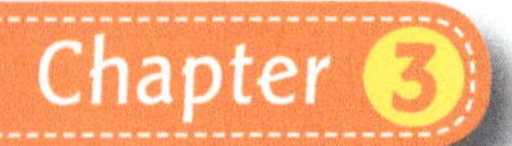

23rd June, 1934

We are in the middle of hard times.
Lots of people can't find jobs.
My dad hasn't worked for two years.

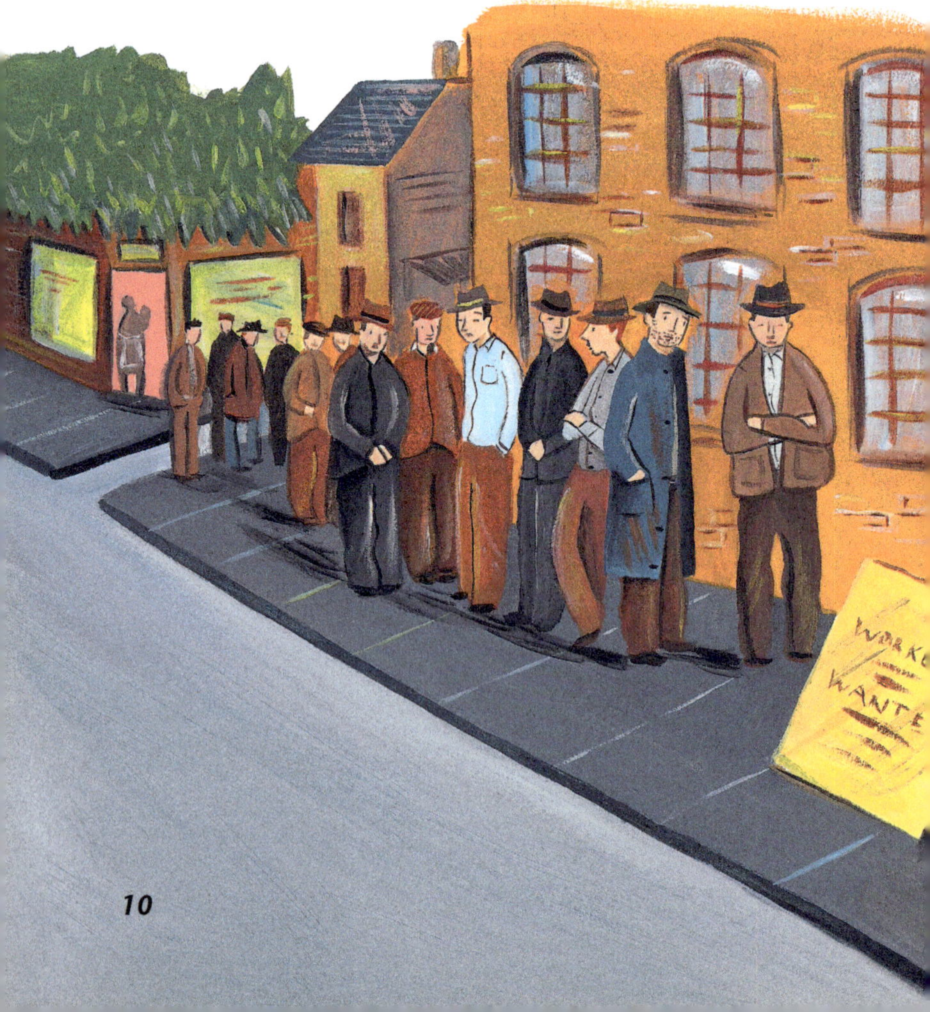

That's why it's so important for me
to take this job.
I can help my family
with the money I make.

When Dad lost his job
we had no money,
so we had to move from our nice house
to this one.

It's really run-down –
hot in summer, and cold in winter.
The paint is coming off the walls.

Rats come up from the cracks
in the floor.
They eat anything.
They've even tried to eat this notebook!

23rd June, 1934

Chapter 4

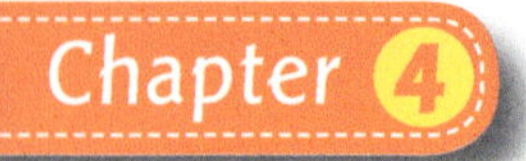

12th October, 1934

When I was at school,
I wanted to leave and go to work.
But now that I am at work,
I miss school.
I miss being with my friends all day.

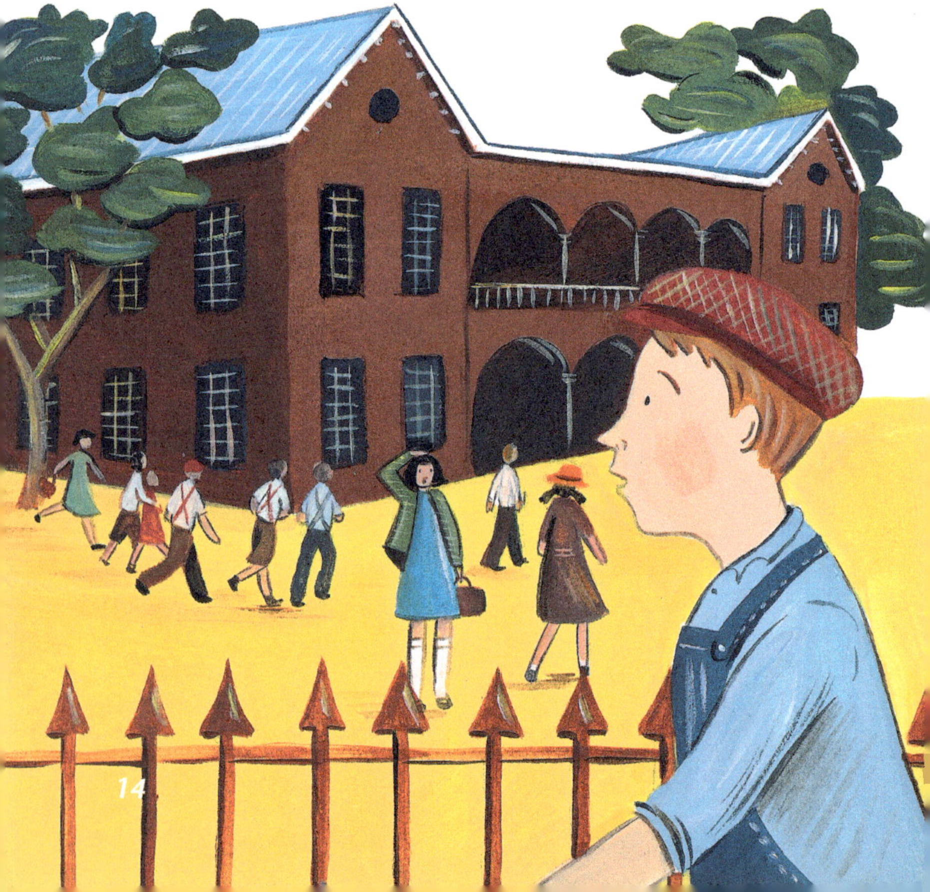

I also miss coming home early and playing games with my brother out on the street.

My work is hard,
and I'm always dirty.
I have to carry wood and bricks all day,
and I can't just stop when I feel like it.

But, mostly, I don't really mind,
because I am learning a lot
about how to make all kinds of things.

Look at this!

Chapter 5

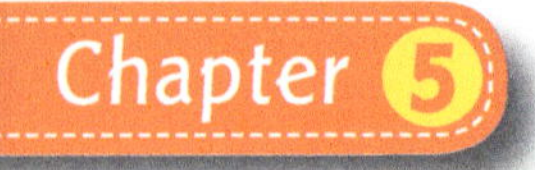

1st May, 1935

I have been in my job
for almost a year now.
I am used to getting up early
and working hard all day.

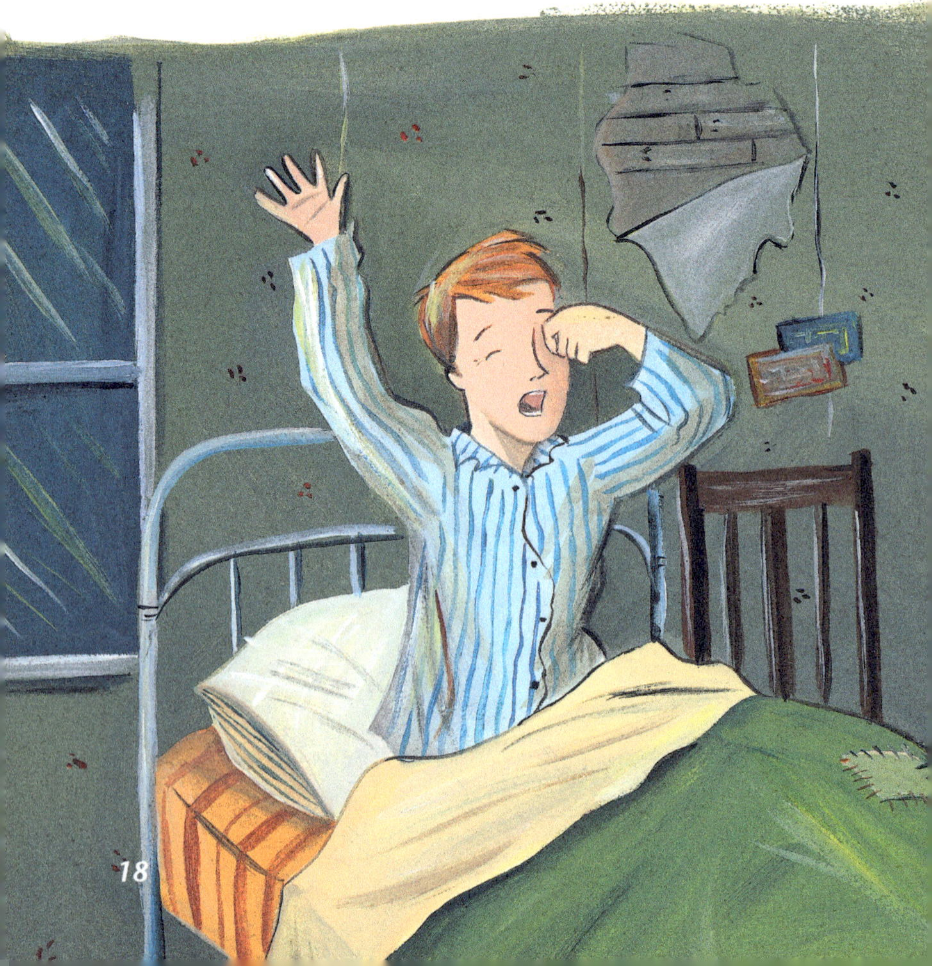

So far, I have helped my boss make five sheds, two houses and a garage.

It's hard to believe,
but Dad got a job last week.
After all these years, he's smiling again.

He says the bad times
are coming to an end,
and things will get better soon.

1st May, 1935

9th May, 1935

I turned fourteen today.
I can't believe that a year has gone by since I stopped school.
I don't miss it so much now, because most of my friends have started working, too.

A few of them came over yesterday,
and we had a small party.
Mum went next door again
to bake the cake.
Dad went out to buy some lemonade.

Chapter 7

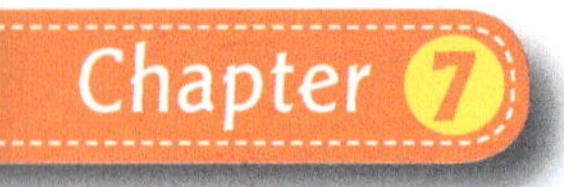

30th October, 1935

Now that Dad is working again, I get to keep some of my own money. On Saturdays, I can go to the movies with my friends.

Things are getting better and better all the time.

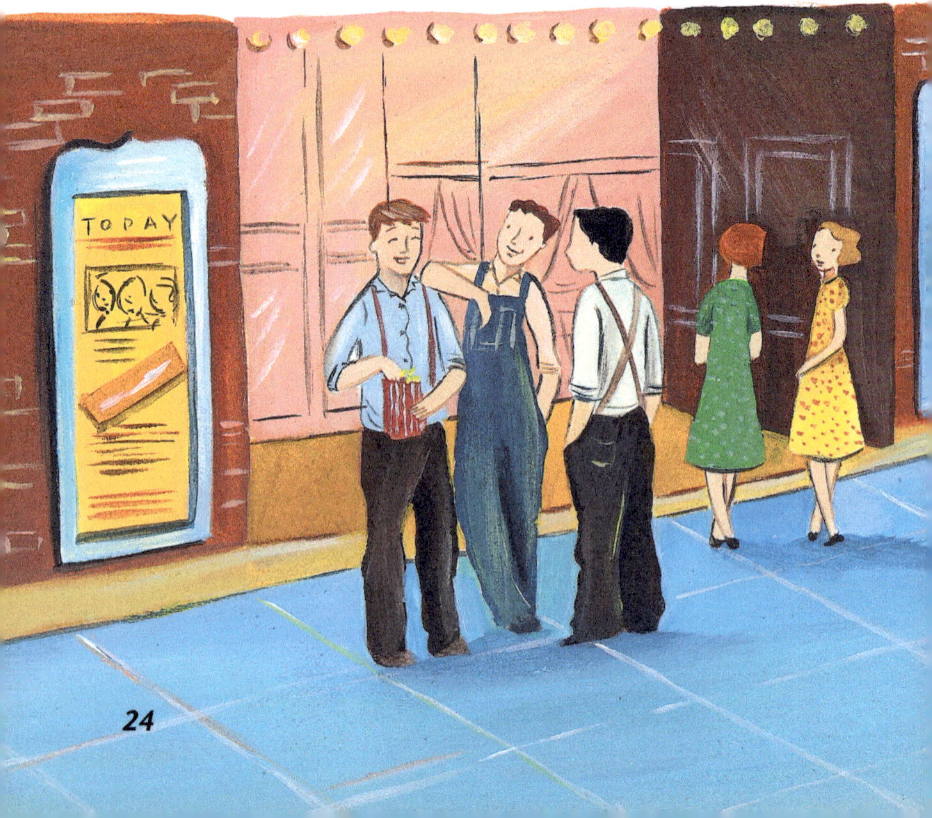